Lessons From The River

A 30 Day Devotional

Lessons From The River
© 2021 Dr. Mel Tavares
Published by SimplyRight Press
ISBN #: 9798664186260

All rights reserved. No part of this book may be reproduced or transmitted in any form or by any means, electronic or mechanical, including photocopying, recording, or by any information storage and retrieval system, without permission in writing from the author.

Scriptures taken from the Holy Bible, New International Version®, NIV®. Copyright © 1973, 1978, 1984, 2011 Used by permission of Zondervan. All rights reserved

"Scripture quotations from the ESV® Bible (The Holy Bible, English Standard Version®), copyright © 2001 by Crossway, a publishing ministry of Good News Publishers. Used by permission. All rights reserved."

Scriptures quotations marked CSB have been taken from the Christian Standard Bible. Copyright 2017 by Holman Bible Publishers. Used by Permisssion.

Scripture quotations marked (CEV) are from the Contemporary English Version Copyright © 1991, 1992, 1995 by American Bible Society. Used by Permission.

Scripture quotations marked (NLT) are taken from the Holy Bible, New Living Translation, copyright ©1996, 2004, 2015 by Tyndale House Foundation. Used by permission of Tyndale House Publishers, Carol Stream, Illinois 60188. All rights reserved.

Scripture quotations marked NASM are taken from the New American Standard Bible. Copyright 1960, 1071, 1977, 1995, 2020. Used by permission. All rights reserved.

The NET Bible, New English Transplantion Copyright 1996 by Bible Studies Press, LLC. Used by permission. All rights reserved.

Scripture quotations from the COMMON ENGLISH BIBLE. © Copyright 2011 COMMON ENGLISH BIBLE. All rights reserved. Used by permission.

Dedication

For the decades I've been going to my favorite river, there has been a wise and faithful man abiding there. His name is Chris Nickerson.

Chris would be the first to say there are two sides to operating Nickerson Park Family Campground. There is the business side (camping) and the ministry side. I would like to speak to the ministry side for a moment. Chris has dedicated himself, his family, and his business to God. He openly speaks of the Lord with those who choose to camp there, be it for a weekend or a season. Sunday church services are held during the summer season at the campground, with the pulpit filled weekly by area pastors. For many years, there has also been a Monday night Bible Study.

He has faithfully poured into countless hundreds (yea thousands?) over the years; ministering to them over the phone, on-site, on the river, along the roads of the campground, or in the lodge. I have been the recipient of Chris's prayers, conversations, and generosity multiple times over the past 20+ years. During one particular period, it was Chris who poured into me there at the river day after day.

It was he who had the vision of doing New England-wide conferences there on the river and he who allowed me to be a part of that team for several years. It was he who first brought my family to Word of Life Campground and years later generously made a way for us to serve with the Connecticut Team at Word of Life, El Salvador. It was he who stood beside me as God launched me into writing for Him, and it was Chris who underwrote the launch of my first book, *Return to Eden: Exposing the Lies Destroying the Family*.

Chris became like a brother to me in so many ways. When I desperately needed direction and healing in a time of brokenness, he talked to me on the river banks and offered hope of the Living Water that was right there for the taking.

It was Chris who walked me down the aisle of the pavilion there on the river and gave me to the man of God's choosing. Marrying Joe meant moving away from the ministry and river that I love so much, and not getting back as frequently as I desire. The lessons of the river remain.

Thank you, Chris, for being a beacon of light in the darkness of people's lives, for always pointing people to the Living Water. Thank you for being my friend, brother, voice of reason over the years, and for allowing me to share the joy and honor of ministering with you, offering life to those who come to the river.

Mel

Table of Contents

Lesson #1	Don't Miss Opportunities
Lesson #2	Watch Out Below
Lesson #3	Predators and Prey
Lesson #4	Ever-flowing Water
Lesson #5	Rise & Fall of the River
Lesson #6	Snagged
Lesson #7	High Waters Recede
Lesson #8	Protective Obstacles
Lesson #9	There's Life in the River
Lesson #10	The Mighty Oaks
Lesson #11	Stagnant in the River
Lesson #12	Be Still
Lesson #13	Sunlight Brings Clarity
Lesson #14	Beware of Snakes
Lesson #15	The River is Multi-Purpose
Lesson #16	In the Heat of the Day
Lesson #17	Sounds of the River
Lesson #18	After the Storm
Lesson #19	Conservation Works
Lesson #20	Respect the Habitat
Lesson #21	Forget the Chaos
Lesson #22	Intimately Acquainted

Lesson #23	Learn From the Experienced
Lesson #24	Power of the Current
Lesson #25	Activity Levels
Lesson #26	Surviving or Thriving
Lesson #27	Sit in Awe
Lesson #28	Community in the River
Lesson #29	Be Prepared
Lesson #30	Experience the River

Life in Jesus, Plain and Simple

About Mel

Day One

Don't Miss Opportunities

When it rains, trickles tumble into the river, adding to the rising waters. As the waters rise and the current increases, a prime opportunity for river tubing is presented. There is a window when the tubing is best, with water high and rapids created as the water rushes over the rocks. The mistake made by many is to put off the opportunity for another time, forgetting the waters will recede just as quickly and opportunity will have passed by.

Isn't that true of life itself? Opportunities present themselves at the most inconvenient times and too often, we let them pass by. It may be a job promotion that means a change of locations. It may be a request to do lead a project and you decline, only to realize later that it was a stepping stone to something greater. Maybe the opportunity was to meet someone for dinner, but it would mean canceling a meeting and driving two hours. It could be an invitation to fish or hike that you decline in favor of doing housework that could have waited.

I'm reminded of the opportunity people had to attend a lavish banquet. Rather than take the opportunity when it came, each came up with a reason why they could not attend. They missed a great opportunity.

Luke 14:16-24 (ESV) But he said to him, "*A man once gave a great banquet and invited many. And at the time for the banquet he sent his servant[a] to say to those who had been invited, 'Come, for everything is now ready.' But they all alike began to make excuses. The first said to him, 'I have bought a field, and I must go out and see it. Please have me excused.' And another said, 'I have bought five yokes of oxen, and I go to examine them. Please have me excused.' And another said, 'I have married a wife, and therefore I cannot come.'"*

Let's not be a part of the crowd who declines invitations and misses opportunities.

Prayer: Lord, thank you for the opportunities you bring my way. May I learn to recognize them and respond quickly; knowing the window of time will not stand open forever. In my scurrying through life, may I not miss all of the good things you desire to give me. Teach me not to miss the moment.

Day Two
Watch Out Below

When river waters are high and moving swiftly, it is impossible to see what lurks below. A novice will merely look at the surface and acknowledge depth is there, with no consideration for what may lie below the surface. Experts who are well acquainted with the river know where the fallen trees and jagged rocks are in a particular bend in the river. Though the objects cannot be seen, the danger is there.

For the unsuspecting in rafts or tubes, in a matter of moments, the tube will pop and they will find themselves in the deep waters. The same holds for the fisherman who does not know the river well. Lures and flies can easily become snagged and left behind to be later discovered by magnet fishermen.

How often do we make similar mistakes in life? We get excited about a particular activity presented for us to join and take the time to consider all of the facets involved. I am reminded of stories of home buyers purchasing merely based on cosmetics and curb appeal. Hasty purchases may prove disastrous, as time reveals electrical, plumbing, and mold issues. A quick decision on a vehicle, a job, or a move across the country may yield similar unwanted results.

Wisdom says we need to be aware of the unseen and recognize dangers below the surface of situations. Failure to take heed will only cause unnecessary consequences.

Proverbs 22:3 (ESV) *"The prudent sees danger and hides himself, but the simple go on and suffer for it."*

May we seek the counsel of others, learn from those who have walked before us, and develop the patience to consider all things carefully, lest we miss important details.

Prayer: Lord, teach me to look below the surface of situations. Help me to judge the whole matter, rather than what is visible to me at a glance. Thank you for giving me the wisdom to avoid those areas where danger lurks below the surface.

Day Three

Predators and Prey

In the river, there are both predators and prey. Depending on the life stage, river creatures are one or the other, or both. Aquatic insects feed on algae or smaller insects. Trout feed on aquatic insects and the heron feeds on the trout. Crayfish lie in wait in the crevice of rock for minnows to swim by and live a contented life. Snapping Turtles feed the crayfish. Such is the circle of life.

Survival depends on the ability to enjoy life and when necessary, obtain life-sustaining food; while simultaneously avoiding the predators who would seek to devour. I immediately think of employment situations we may find ourselves in.

Ideally, you work in a job that you thoroughly enjoy and in an environment of like-minded people. In many workplaces, there is at least one predator who is jealous and wants your position or feels the need to attack you to make themselves look better. It is the way of the world.

Our response is not to treat them poorly, but that we remember the battle is not about flesh and blood but is about the enemy of our souls who will all manner of opportunity to prey on us.

Ephesians 6:12 (ESV) *"For we do not wrestle against flesh and blood, but against the rulers, against the authorities, against the cosmic powers over this present darkness, against the spiritual forces of evil in the heavenly places."*

You may have a family member or a friend or neighbor who seems to be constantly picking fights. Their sole purpose in life seems to be to do all they can to bring you down. Remember that it really isn't them who has the issue with you. It is Satan using the situation in an attempt to destroy you. Be on guard.

1 Peter 5:8 (ESV)*"Be sober-minded; be watchful. Your adversary the devil prowls around like a roaring lion, seeking someone to devour."*

Prayer: "Lord, teach me to be aware of my surroundings while I live this life you have given to me. Teach me not to be vulnerable and guard me against becoming prey to the enemy of my soul."

Day Four
Ever-flowing Water

The water here at the river is ever-flowing. When the rains come and the waters rise, the river flows more swiftly. When the drought comes and the river is at times but a trickle, watch carefully. The water does not sit stagnantly. It is still flowing and there is still life in the water. So it should be with us. There are seasons in our lives when everything is lush and green and life is good. Rivers of living water flow out of us easily.

Other seasons in our life are drier and the rivers of living water are not as apparent in our lives. Circumstances of life have weighed us down and begun to dry up the waters. The scorching sun has evaporated the strength of the flow.

Often times, we are so busy that we don't realize how parched we are. In the natural and in the spiritual, long stretches with no in-filling of water cause pain and unclear thinking. It is then that we become weak.

Just as fresh rains once again fill the river beds and allow the water to flow at a higher capacity, the Holy Spirit desires to fill us anew and afresh so that rivers of living water once again course through our veins and overflow to those around us who are desperate for a touch from God. If we are thirsty, we must go to the living water, ever-flowing and ever waiting for us to come.

John 7:37-38 (ESV) *"On the last day of the feast, the great day, Jesus stood up and cried out, "If anyone thirsts, let him come to me and drink. Whoever believes in me, as the Scripture has said, 'Out of his heart will flow rivers of living water.'"*

Prayer: Lord, I am in a dry spot. I long to be vibrant once again, filled and overflowing. You said if anyone is thirsty, to come to you and you would provide the living waters. I pray as I sit and soak up your presence and as you fill me, may rivers of living waters flow out of me once again, overflowing to the lives around me once again.

Day Five
Rise & Fall of the River

Have you ever watched the river rise? One day of heavy rain and the river visibly rises. If your vantage point is downstream, the waters rise even higher because of the trickles running into the river upstream. As it travels downstream the intensity grows. I've been at the river when there's been a deluge of rain for several days and the waters rise to flood stage. I've also witnessed a similar rise in the waters when spring run-off occurs as the snow melts.

As surely as the river rises, the river will fall. It's one of the curious ways of creation that draws me to the river. Many times when I spend a weekend camping at the river, I witness this phenomenon. On one particular trip, it had rained for two days before my arrival. To me, that meant a prime opportunity to go river tubing that first day. Why the first day? Because I knew the waters would begin to fall over the next two days and provide a much slower ride than day one.

A working knowledge of the ways of the river is critical to those who live along the river. Although there are times of disaster (like a dam breaking upstream), typically one intimately acquainted with the ways of the river will watch the waters carefully and respond accordingly.

The same goes for us in life. Often, there are patterns in our lives. The job wears on us and we build up emotions and then spew them at home. We worry ourselves sick about the future, losing much needed sleep at night. Some struggle with bitterness and unforgiveness, resulting in the development of ulcers and other diseases.

All of these 'rising waters' can be avoided. If we watch carefully, we will recognize the patterns in ourselves and others, be prepared for the rising waters and sound the warning for others.

Ezekial 38:7(CSB)"*Be prepared and get yourself ready, you and your whole assembly that has been mobilized around you; you will be their guard.*"

Prayer: Lord, teach me the ways of the rising and falling of the waters of life. Help me to be prepared for the days the waters will rise and help me to sound the alarm to others, that they also may be prepared.

Day Six
Snagged

If you were to dive to the bottom of the river, you would see all types of tackle snagged in the crevices of rocks and the submerged branches. They serve as a reminder that dangers often lurk in dark waters, hidden by shadows or by the depth of the water.

When a fisherman gets snagged on the bottom, the first thing he will do is attempt to free the tackle. As he moves around, moves his pole, reels to and fro, he hopes that his expensive lure will break free. If not, a choice must be made. He will either go into the water after it, or he will cut the line and his losses. For those willing and able to recover the snagged tackle, there is now another chance to pursue using it for the purpose for which it was created-to lure fish to the hook.

Likewise, we hit snags in life. Just as the fisherman casts only to find himself snagged on the bottom, we can set out in a direction and run into unexpected snags. Perhaps you've decided to do a home improvement project but your plans are being held up because of zoning boards and permits. Like the fisherman, you have to decide whether to push all-in or abandon the idea and walk away.

Often, the snags are emotional or spiritual in nature. I know of many who get entangled in the unseen when pursuing a passion or purpose. Sadly, too often I witness people give up when they hit a snag. It may be the musician who didn't make the audition cut, the teacher who didn't get the position or the entrepreneur who can't break into the market. Just as it is easier for the fisherman to cut the line and walk away, these gifted passionate individuals give up and walk away from purpose.

We should be turning to the Lord to give us strength and make a way when plans don't work out and we hit snags along the way. Rest assured that He is there to guide us and to help us persevere with determination, not allowing snags to cause us to give up. Philippians 4:13 (CEV)"*Christ gives me strength to face anything.*"

Prayer: Dear God, help me to remember that snags are a normal part of the process of pursuing passion and purpose. When temptation comes to just cut my losses and walk away, give me the strength to persevere.

Day Seven

High Waters Recede

As surely as waters rise, they will recede. Sometimes waters get very high, nearing flood stage and threatening to spill over the banks. When severe storms come, waters rise beyond flood stage and indeed spill the banks. Typically, there are warnings that the rising waters will surpass flood stage, and sometimes there is little warning. When the high waters come, for a time everything is engulfed below the waters. Sometimes the waters quietly and rise, deceiving the untrained eye. Sometimes the water rises quickly, flowing fast and furious.

Whatever the situation that causes the waters to rise and whatever the manner of the rising, the outcomes are the same. The waters are high and everything in the path is submerged for a season. There's the key thought. 'For a season.' As surely as the waters rise, the river will crest and the high waters will begin to recede. It is important to remember that high waters recede more slowly than they rise, depending on variables such as the temperature, winds, and continued rainfall.

Likewise, the storms in our lives may cause waters to rise temporarily. We may find ourselves overwhelmed by the high waters, but it is important to remember that the water level will change and the situation will change. Variables of our situation will impact how quickly the waters recede, but they will recede! Rest and be peaceful in the midst of it all, and know that Jesus is the master of the wind.

Matthew 8:24-27 (NIV) *Suddenly a furious storm came up on the lake so that the waves swept over the boat. But Jesus was sleeping. The disciples went and woke him, saying, "Lord, save us! We're going to drown!" He replied, "You of little faith, why are you so afraid?" Then he got up and rebuked the winds and the waves, and it was completely calm. The men were amazed and asked, "What kind of man is this? Even the winds and the waves obey him!"*

Prayer: Lord Jesus, help me to remember that you are the master of the wind and you control the storms of life. Help me to rest and be peaceful in the midst of the storm and trust you, knowing the situation will change soon and the high waters will recede.

Day Eight
Protective Obstacles

Many people love tubing, kayaking, and even canoeing rivers. One weekend not long ago, I went camping along my favorite river, with the intent of sitting back and relaxing on the river for a weekend. Yet, I found myself as busy as ever, cooking and cleaning up the site and not taking time to relax.

The river provides immense opportunities for whoever will partake of the waters. At some point, I decided to go tubing, but in my typical Type A Personality fashion checked my phone and decided it would need to be a quick trip before I started lunch. I hopped into the tube and headed down the river. Much to my dismay, I encountered obstacle after obstacle, some above the surface and some below. My journey time downriver was double what I planned, as I was forced to slow down and follow the course of the river.

Admittedly, I was slightly anxious about lunch being delayed. As I disembarked and made my way back to my site, it occurred to me that the river obstacles were protective, forcing me to slow down and live at a slower pace as well as observe the details of the river. Was anyone really going to starve if I didn't put lunch on the table at a certain time? (The truth was, no one cared but me.)

How many times do we hurry through our days and seasons of life, frustrated when obstacles get in the way of our plans and timelines? We would do well to tune in to the ways of the living water(the living God) and realize that sometimes He places obstacles in our path for our protection, allowing us time to rest.

Mark 6:31-32 (NIV) *"Then, because so many people were coming and going that they did not even have a chance to eat, he said to them, 'Come with me by yourselves to a quiet place and get some rest.' So they went away by themselves in a boat to a solitary place."*

Prayer: Lord, may I recognize the obstacles you place before me are for my protection, to allow me to slow down and attend to myself and my time with you first.

Day Nine
There's Life in the River

The river is full of life. In my favorite river, there are trout of all sizes as well as an occasional salmon that was stocked in a lake upstream and likely made its way into the river during heavy rains. River life isn't limited to fish however; the novice will miss the smaller and less noticeable life. Hidden amongst the rocks are crayfish, all types of nearly imperceptible insects, and frogs. Even smaller are the hatches of browns, stoneflies, and caddis. There is a wide variety of vegetation growing both in the river and along the banks. There is life in the river.

   Life in the river is varied and comes in many forms, and there is no mistaking the reality of the waters being healthy and providing the environment necessary to thrive in the river. Even when the water levels drop, there is life in the river. Some creatures find a deeper hole, a smaller trickle, or a cool riverbank under the cleft of a rock to take refuge during times of drought. Sadly, some creatures will die during the drought, unwilling to adapt and move from where they typically reside.

John 4:10 (ESV)"*If you knew the gift of God, and who it is that is saying to you, 'Give me a drink,' you would have asked him, and he would have given you living water.*"

Jesus refers to himself as Living Water and Scriptures refer to the Holy Spirit as providing rivers of living water to all who will come and partake. We have the opportunity to dwell in the river of life, thriving during times of drought. There, we will find other living beings, also thriving as they dwell in the living waters. Regardless of how dire our circumstances, how difficult of drought we find ourselves in, we can go to the freely offered river filled with life.

Prayer: Lord Jesus, I know you are the living water that I need. I know there life is found in you. Not just life, but abundant life. May I always live in the river flowing and filled with life.

Day Ten

The Mighty Oaks

Have you ever sat in in the summer shade of the mighty oaks lining the river bank? I once sat sipping my coffee and listening to the babbling of rapids and considered the trees I was sitting under. Being well-acquainted with the ways of this particular river, I reflected on the number of times waters had flooded this section of the land, yet the mighty oaks remain standing.

I considered how many years, including this current year, when drought has dried up much vegetation, including trees with shallow roots. Yet, the mighty oaks remain green and acorns are forming.

Storms rage through this part of the state and often result in the uprooting of many trees, but not the mighty oak. Multiple heatwaves have not suffocated the mighty oaks, for their roots are deep into the soil of the river banks and perhaps extend out into the deep of the river bed itself.

The mighty oak trees have stood strong through the decades. Can we say the same? Are our roots deep, deep into the soil of the Lord? Or, do we begin to wither when the heat gets turned up in our lives? Do we withstand storms that will surely come, or do we exit the storms tattered and torn?

Do we fear the future, or do we trust that we will continue bearing fruit during the drought and hard times we are seeing in this world? The answer is to learn from the mighty oak and plant ourselves by the Living Water and allow our roots to go deep and deeper still.

Jeremiah 17:8 (ESV) *"He is like a tree planted by water, that sends out its roots by the stream, and does not fear when heat comes, for its leaves remain green, and is not anxious in the year of drought, for it does not cease to bear fruit."*

Prayer: Father, I ask that you teach me to sit and drink of the Living Water, that I may grow as a mighty oak of righteousness, fearing nothing and bearing much fruit; even during the storms of life that are sure to come.

Day Eleven
Stagnant in the River

Have you noticed that water in the river becomes stagnant as the season progresses? The reason is simple. As the current and water flow decrease, certain sections get very little movement. Algae begin to build up and it becomes a breeding ground for mosquitoes. Fish love to hide under the riverbank, unaware they become easy prey for the heron or the snapping turtle. The water begins to smell and becomes opposite the beauty of a flowing river tumbling over the rocks.

We can become stagnant in life and begin to give off a foul odor and appearance if we step out of the flow of the Holy Spirit and the life God has intended for us. At first, it may not be obvious we are beginning to stagnate. Careful consideration will cause us to realize things are more cloudy than usual. Cloudiness will turn to confusion and we will find answers don't come easily.

Worse yet, left unattended our stagnation will turn to negative attitudes, depression, and poor decisions. Direction is lacking. We are lacking the flow of knowledge and wisdom that a life lived for God brings to us. We become a stench to God, rather than a blessing. Isaiah 65:5(b) (NLT) says *"These people become a stench to my nostrils, an acrid smell that never goes away."*

Just as rains bring refreshment and the stagnant water begins to flow in the river again, so it is that we can spend time with God, reading His Word and the flow will begin again. The more we connect with God, the more the rivers of Living Water will flow through us. John 7:38 (NASB) *"Whoever believes in me, as the Scripture has said, from his innermost being will flow rivers of living water."*

We are designed to be filled with life that we may be active and moving, doing those things God has created us to do. As the rivers (of God) flow through us, we will manifest the fruit of the Spirit (Galatians 5:22) and be effective and successful in our endeavors.

Prayer: Heavenly Father, I pray for rivers of living water to begin to flow through me again. Forgive me for allowing my life to become stagnant. My desire is for the waters to flow, that I may be used to bring life to others downstream.

Day Twelve
Be Still

The phrase 'sitting beside of the still waters' is often misinterpreted and thought to be direction for us to sit near a glassy calm lake, as opposed to moving water. It is important to note that the Hebrew translation for the phrase '*still waters*' is '*waters of rest*'. Indeed the river is a water of rest. Sitting beside the still waters of the flowing river, one can breathe deeply and take in every sound of the water cresting over rocks and dropping below, of the occasional fish splashing as it jumps, the leaves rustling in the breeze, and the birds chirping.

Forgetting all of the clutter and matters that consume us and clamor for our attention, our souls can be refreshed and restored at the river. Restoration involves reflection. When we slow down enough to just reflect on our lives from God's perspective, we can rest in knowing we are loved, protected, and cared for by God. When we slow down, we have time to think, evaluate, and assess. Our brains process better in the quiet and stillness.

It is in the place of rest that we become quiet enough to hear the voice of God. It isn't that He doesn't speak at other times, but so often we do not hear His voice because of our frenzied days being filled going to and fro. It is easy to become overwhelmed with daily life and storms that come our way and yet how often do we remember to stop and be still and talk to the Lord? If we are in need, we can pray and ask God to meet those. He is our shepherd, we shall not want.

Psalm 23:1-3 (ESV) *"The Lord is my shepherd; I shall not want. He makes me lie down in green pastures. He leads me beside still waters. He restores my soul. He leads me in paths of righteousness (the right path) for his name's sake."*

Prayer: Lord, teach me to rest beside the still waters. Help me to breathe deeply and take in the sounds of your creation while shutting out all of the other noise. Speak to me in the quiet place of rest.

Day Thirteen
Sunlight Brings Clarity

Cloudy days, shady overhangs, and darkness all create challenges in seeing the contents of the river clearly. One is left to imagine what might be there, whether positive or negative. Have you ever been fishing and lost a lure on a log lying on the river bottom and invisible in the shadows? I have. I've also hit rocks while tubing at dusk and realized that while I thought I knew the river well enough to avoid them, my memory faded. Cloud covers often make it impossible to see the bottom, even if the water is only a few feet deep.

When the sun comes out, clarity shines brightly. Suddenly, the bottom can be seen. Looking down, one can see the fish swimming around, the rocks are obvious, and fallen logs are visible once again. The unseen becomes seen.

The same concept holds true in life. Storms come. Clouds and shadows loom as night closes in. Often we see realities dimly as we look with our human eyes at circumstances. Our judgment is clouded by emotions that prove to be fickle friends, and we lose our sense of direction. Yet, when we look to the Lord, SONlight shines upon us, and clarity is given.

Friends are great for being honest with us and giving us a fresh perspective. How many times has a friend or family member listened to you and then said "Well, I don't see it quite the same." They then proceed to give their view, often resulting in you getting clarity in the situation.

If we dive into the Bible in search of truth, we find clarity. If we pray and seek wisdom and counsel from the Holy Spirit, we can see things with the proper perspective. Psalm 25:4 (NIV) *"Show me your ways, Lord, teach me your paths."* We need God to teach us.

Prayer: Lord, I realize there are times I see dimly amid my circumstances, in the swirl of challenges and storms life often brings. I ask that you show me your ways, Lord. Shine your light brightly into my clouded world and the shadows, that I may see reality with clarity and not be deceived as to what truth is.

Day Fourteen
Beware of Snakes

There is life in the river. We often approach the river with enthusiasm, anxious to partake of all it has to offer. If camping, the site is barely set up before tubes and rafts are filled and launched into the river. Fishermen cast their lines into the water, determined to lure fish swimming in search of food.

When I am at the river, it is not uncommon to suddenly hear an unsuspecting visitor yell. I instinctively know that they've encountered a snake.

In Connecticut, the Northern Water Snake frequents freshwater lakes and streams. Often mistaken for the poisonous black water moccasin, this snake is not poisonous. Typically, the snakes swim the river close to the banks, sniffing out their prey of fish, frogs, crayfish, and insects. Snakes prey on the life that we are also seeking. Their keen sense of smell and vision causes them to leave their resting place along the banks and quickly slither below the water at the first indication of being discovered.

Only those river lovers who spend time observing and learning the ways of the river are aware that seen or unseen, the snakes reside with the river life and exist to prey on the unsuspecting creatures. Likewise, Satan lives to prey on us. Seen or unseen, he's ever watching for the opportunity to devour those not keeping watch. Carefully study of the ways of the snake will allow us to anticipate his whereabouts and be prepared to deal with it.

1 Peter 5:8 (ESV) *"Be sober-minded; be watchful. Your adversary the devil prowls around like a roaring lion, seeking someone to devour"*

Prayer: Lord, thank you for giving me eyes to see dangers and traps that are set before me. Thank you for protecting me from the efforts of my enemy (Satan/Devil) who prowls around like a roaring lion, who watches and waits for the unsuspecting person. Thank you that I have no reason to fear and that you've given me the weapons I need to stay safe, but at the same time, let me never forget the snakes (Satan)are always nearby, seen or unseen.

Day Fifteen
The River is Multi-Dimensional

The river is multi-dimensional. It is first and foremost, the sustainer of life for all who live there. Without the river existing, none of the created life can exist. If the river dies, all dependent creatures will also die. The river functions as the life-giver. The river provides an opportunity for rest and relaxation. Those who come to the river can unwind while fishing, kayaking, or tubing the river. Others might come to the banks to reflect on all the river has to offer, how powerful and magnificent it is, and rest in those realities.

The multi-dimensional attributes of God provide the same diversity as a river does. As our desires and needs change over time, they can still be met by the same entity. There is no need to search elsewhere as He is our all in all. Within the triune Godhead exists the Father, the Son, and the Holy Spirit. This complexity is the simplicity of functions.

Within the Godhead, we have a Savior, a teacher, a counselor, creator, and sustainer. When we need rest, He is our peace. When we are sick, He is our healer. He is the rock we can cling to when storms come and waters rise. He is the Fisher of Men and is always luring us to Himself, longing to draw us nearer and nearer still. He is El Shaddai, our Most High God, who nourishes us and is more than sufficient. (El means God and Shaddai means sufficiency, sustenance, blessing, and nourishment.) He is all we need, regardless of the circumstances we find ourselves in on any given day.

2 Samuel 22:32-34 (NIV) *"For who is God besides the LORD? And who is the Rock except our God? It is God who arms me with strength and makes my way secure. He makes my feet like the feet of a deer; he enables me to stand on the heights."*

Psalm 54:4 (NIV) *"Surely God is my help; the Lord is the one who sustains me."*

Prayer: Thank you, God that you are all I need. That within you I find life, security, and strength. Thank you for being the rock that anchors me in the storms of life, for being water to my thirsty soul, for being the Bread of Life, for giving me joy and laughter, and rest when I am weary. Help me to come to you each day, and allow you to be all I need for that day.

Day Sixteen

In the Heat of the Day

When the unforgiving sun beats down relentlessly, the river offers a refreshing refuge. The water is cool and offers a reprieve to swimmers and rafters. Often the cool water creates an atmosphere of deception and those partaking of water cooler than the air are left exposed to the sun. Uncaring about water or air temperatures, the UV rays of the sun scorches throughout the heat of the day.

Shallow waters become too warm for fish and other living creatures to endure, and they move to the cooler waters along the river banks, sheltered by overhanging rocks, trees, and vegetation. Wise people soon follow suit and find refuge in a bottle of sunscreen or the shadows of the banks.

An analogy can be drawn of our spiritual lives. We are wise to live a life surrendered to Christ, filled with prayer and praise. It is in the secret place of abiding, we can take shelter under the wings of the Almighty. There under the wings, we are protected and can continue to thrive, even when we find ourselves in the unrelenting heat of the day. It is not automatic protection, just as there isn't a shift in the natural of trees extending their branches to protect people and creatures in the river. Action is required on our part to move into the protective shadow, lest we be exposed to the heat of the day.

Psalm 91:1 (CEV)"*Live under the protection of God Most High and stay in the shadow of God All-Powerful."*

Prayer: Lord, teach me to abide in the secret place, communing with you throughout my days. Thank you for providing shelter under your wings of protection for all who choose to abide with you. Thank you for providing a reprieve from the heat of the days we face. I know that left unsheltered, many of the fiery trials would scorch and consume me, but you O Lord, are faithful to keep your promises to those of us who abide in you.

Day Seventeen
Sounds of the River

A well-tuned ear recognizes the sounds of the river. As the river fills during rain, the sound of the river changes and becomes more muted in some areas as rocks are covered and no longer allow water to babble over them. Yet, downriver a set of rapids will swell from a Class I to a Class IV whitewater, given enough rain.

Whitewater forms when the gradient significantly changes and causes a turbulent current angrily frothing its way through the river. The danger exists when an ear hears rising waters and is a signal to move to higher ground as the banks will frequently overflow and carry bystanders with the swift current.

As surely as it rises, the river will fall. Raging waters will recede and rocks recently invisible will begin to protrude through the surface. The trained ear discerns the shift in the current speed and hears the change in water coursing over rocks. Babbling spots are heard once again. As the water gently spills over the rocks, birds can again be heard chirping in the nearby trees. If much time is spent on the river, a person becomes intimately acquainted with every nuance and quickly picks up on new sounds, imperceptible to the casual listener. Closer inspection may reveal a recently fallen tree in the river or a new path carved by the recent flood.

The river is representative of our lives. If we are tuned in, we hear the warnings from God when storms bring rising waters and prepare accordingly. As we spend time with Him daily, we become intimately acquainted with the gentle voice of the Lord and are sensitive to the slightest changes.

Genesis 3:8 (NIV) *"Then the man and his wife heard the sound of the Lord God as he was walking in the garden in the cool of the day..."*

Prayer: Oh Lord God, thank you that all of these centuries later, we can hear the sound of you as we sit or walk in the cool of the day. Thank you that you desire we walk and talk with you and become intimately acquainted with your voice that sometimes will serve as a warning to us, and sometimes as a soothing and calming directional voice of love and assurance.

Day Eighteen
After the Storm

Whether you temporarily or permanently live along the river, it is important to inspect and assess the status of the river daily. If there are storms, it is important to assess them during the storm but it is also critical to assess them after the storm.

It is during the hours and days following the end of a storm that the greatest danger exists, for it is then that some people think it is safe and let their guard down. With guards down, those below fail to notice trees precariously dangling, until another breeze comes and shakes the broken branches loose and crashing to the ground.

Unguarded hearts may joyfully jump into the full river for a post-storm raft ride, only to be stranded by a sharp rock that burst the raft. Those happy to get back to fishing may fall straight into the water, having never considered the danger of the wet and slippery rocks on the river bank.

It is imperative to stay guarded and continue praying after the storm has passed by. Tensions built during the storm may prematurely be released causing the unintended shift. We can slip and fall quickly if we don't take time to stabilize after a storm. The more challenging and damaging the storm, the longer it will take us to regain a sure footing. Our worlds may still be (proverbially) spinning and we need to re-center before making decisions or taking action in a particular direction. We re-center and guarded through prayer.

Phil. 4:6-7 (ESV) *"Do not be anxious about anything, but in everything by prayer and supplication with thanksgiving let your requests be made known to God. And the peace of God, which surpasses all understanding, will guard your hearts and your minds in Christ Jesus."*

Prayer: Lord God, thank you that you are with me in the storm and also after the storm passes by. Thank you for protecting against unseen dangers and guiding me, that my feet will not stumble and my heart will not fail.

Day Nineteen
Conservation Works

Abiding by conservation principles keeps the water pure, untainted, and clear. Most rivers I visit are clean and free of man's trash. There have been some that I've visited that are very deep, yet I can see to the bottom. Others I've visited are dirty and so murky I cannot see a foot down. What is the difference? It's all about conservation and those who are willing to follow the rules.

Proper care along the river banks helps keep soil from eroding. Not protecting the vegetation causes soil to wash into the river and the sediment to create unclear runoff. Runoff can sometimes come from further back on the property. For example, if a vehicle is washed uphill of the river bed, chemicals used to wash often make their way into the water.

Likewise, chemical sprays used to kill undesired vegetation and insects often make their way into the waterway. The same holds for pet waste. Following the rules along the river keeps it clean and pure for everyone to enjoy as the river thrives. When principles are not followed and a waterway becomes polluted, a long process of clean-up and restoration must be implemented.

Similarly, if we abide by the principles found in the Bible, our hearts remain pure and untainted. Just as one would not necessarily think that washing vehicles uphill could pollute the river, we do not always consider an action or thought could pollute our hearts and minds. Anger, pride, envy, jealousy, arguments, and discontentment all pollute us.

Thankfully, their clean-up and restoration need not be as long of a process as river clean-up is. All that is required is that we admit that we have allowed these things to pollute us (aka we've sinned) and ask God to purify us and restore us to our original state of cleanliness.

Psalm 51:10 (ESV) *"Create in me a clean heart, O God, and renew a right spirit within me."*

1 John 1:9 (NIV) *"If we confess our sins, He is faithful and just and will forgive us of our sins and purify us from all unrighteousness."*

Prayer: Oh God, I see that my heart has become polluted. I've allowed attitudes and actions to creep in and muddy the waters of my soul. I ask that you forgive me and create in me a clean heart.

Day Twenty
Respect the Habitat

Few things soothe a soul like the babbling sound of the river. It is teeming with life, including fish that are there for our enjoyment, both as catch/release and as dinner that evening. Did God intend for us to eat the fish? I believe so. Leviticus 1:9 (NET) confirms my conviction "*These you can eat from all creatures that are in the water: Any creatures in the water that have both fins and scales, whether in the seas or the streams, you may eat.*"

Whether for catch and release purposes or to enjoy as a meal, fish will only continue to thrive in the river if the habitat remains unpolluted. I've witnessed too many once-thriving rivers that are a little better than the dead sea now. The erosion of the habitat is typically a slow process, perhaps starting with trash being left to find its way into the current before settling on the bottom. A careless spill of a toxin, a mindless act of pet waste being left near the river bank to wash into the stream, or pesticides sprayed nearby and the habitat becomes compromised.

The same is true of our lives. If we are not careful to guard and protect our health against pollutants, it is very easy for our habitat to become off-balance.

We must take care to nurture our spirit, mind, and body. The great thing about the river is it provides the perfect environment to restore balance to our lives. Jesus often took time by himself to retreat from the noisy crowds and busyness of life. One example is found in Mark 1:35 (NIV) *"It was very early in the morning and still dark. Jesus got up and left the house. He went to a place where he could be alone and he prayed."*

Sitting and listening to the sounds of the birds, watching the fish pool and jump and endeavoring to catch one if desired, and enjoying the never-ending sound of the water running across the rocks will soothe your stress away.

Prayer: Lord God, thank you for the creation you have given us to enjoy. Thank you for the wisdom to know when I need to just stop and rest for a while and enjoy the river. Help me to guard against letting the cares of this world pollute my spirit, mind, and body. May I find rest for my soul today.

Day Twenty-One
Forget the Chaos

Another way to think of restoration is to re-align priorities before we go back to our daily lives, determined to live less chaotically. Defined, the cares of this world include our jobs, our homes, our possessions, and anything else that causes us to live less than peaceful lives. If we do not guard our time and energy carefully, the pursuit of more and the cares of this world will steal our rest. Sitting beside the still waters, you will find the rest you so desperately need.

Mark 4:19 (ESV) *"But the cares of the world and the deceitfulness of riches and the desires for other things enter in and choke the word, and proves unfruitful."*

The great thing about life on the river is there is no need for technology. I encourage you to leave your phone alone for the day or the weekend and just enjoy being in nature. Build a campfire and sit and listen to it crackle. Grab a tube and drift down the river for a couple of hours. Grab your fish pole and try to lure a trout to your line. Go for a walk along the riverbanks. Pull up a chair and sit by the waters for a while. Whatever your choice of unplugged relaxation, use the time to reflect on how you are feeling right now compared to when you arrived at the river.

What is making the difference? Is it possible to retain some of the peace and calmness when you leave the river? The answer is yes, with an intentional effort.

Finding a peaceful and restful place at home is one way to avoid the feelings of chaos in your daily life. I have a tabletop fire bowl that I light often, which replaces the campfires I love so much. A half-hour of sipping coffee and staring at the fire does wonders for the soul. I also invested in a couple of inexpensive table-top fountains that (albeit poorly) mimic the water babbling over rocks at the river.

Think about what might work for you and take just a few minutes to close your eyes and escape the chaos of the day.

Prayer: Lord, show me those things that are stealing my peace and causing me stress in my day-to-day life. Help me to find ways to let things go and re-prioritize where possible. Show me how to take some of the peace and calm with me when I leave the river, that my life may be carefree and filled with abundant joy.

Day Twenty-Two
Become Intimately Acquainted

Whether you intend to tube, fish, or catch the perfect photo of the heron that calls the river his home, your intimate knowledge of the river will determine your success. The more you learn all of the characteristics of the river as it rises and falls through the seasons, the more you will see the intimate details that escape the eyes of the majority.

Knowing the river during the dry seasons means you know where the large rocks are when the heavy rains come. The rocks that once protruded are the same that will snag the tube of an unsuspecting rider caught up in the thrill of the swift waters. Knowing the river intimately means you know the fallen tree in the river bend is a refuge for trout and a treasure-trove of expensive fishing lures for newcomers who are unaware of the submerged tree. Carefully studying the patterns of the heron means you will have your camera ready when he comes upriver to fish in the late afternoon.

The same analogy is true of our knowledge with God. The better acquainted we are with Him, the more we can take refuge and enjoy the benefits few ever tap into. As we spend time with Him reading the Bible, praying, and communing with Him, the more will be revealed to us. We will know His character intimately and mysteries will be revealed.

Matthew 13:11 (ESV) *"Jesus answered them, "To you, it has been granted to know the mysteries of the kingdom of heaven, but to them, it has not been granted."*

God wants us to know the deeper things that are not obvious to casual observers and give us insight if we would search.

Just as the fisherman must learn the ways of the fish and the ways of the river, each of us must search and learn for ourselves. Me telling a newcomer to the river about deep holes and lures will only give a glimpse into how to fish the river. Once the newcomer begins fishing and studying for himself, he will develop a deeper understanding of the mysterious ways of the fish.

Prayer: Lord, I want to know you. I want to understand the deeper things of your Kingdom. Just as you've given the ability for me to understand the ways of the river and life therein, you've given me the promise to reveal mysteries most will never notice. I ask that you give me an understanding of things unseen.

Day Twenty-Three
Learn From the Experienced

My dad taught me long ago that I could learn from those who'd already gone before me or I could just stumble forward myself and learn the hard way. He was quick to point out that many sufferings, hardships, and mistakes could be avoided by learning from the experienced rather than having pride in doing it myself with no help from anyone. So it is on the river. Wisdom says it is better to learn from those who are experienced.

Experienced fisherman will know when the browns hatch and when the caddis is about to hatch and which flies will work at what time of the day. Those who fish with lures can help you determine which lures to use when the water is high and which to use when the water is much lower. Avid fishermen know that early morning and dusk are better for fishing, and daytime is best left to those wanting to swim or tube.

Ask those who are well acquainted with the river about the best spots and tips regarding what lurks below the water in certain sections of the water. There's no shame in learning from someone else. After all, if you are seeking the best experience and making the most of your time, why waste it learning the hard way?

In our work lives, we learn our jobs from those who've been in the field longer than us. When driving from one point to another, many of us use a GPS and depend on the system creators to know to direct us to our destination. Why then, would we try to navigate our personal and spiritual lives without using a similar roadmap?

Consider Isaiah 58:11 (NIV). *"And the LORD will guide you continually and satisfy your desire in scorched places and make your bones strong; and you shall be like a watered garden, like a spring of water, whose waters do not fail."*

The Bible gives us clear direction for life situations and how to live, how to make decisions, what to do, and what to avoid. It is to our benefit to learn from their experiences, both negative and positive rather than unnecessarily making mistakes and suffering hardships.

Prayer: Lord, thank you for the Biblical accounts and experiences of the many who have gone before me. May I study these accounts and learn from them Thank you for the people you surround me with each day.

Day Twenty-Four
Power of the Current

Have you ever sat and watched a river flow and noticed the power in the current? The higher the water after a rain below a dam, the stronger the current is. Even when a river is low and appears to be still, it is still moving and there is still a current. Along the banks and in the eddy's are often areas of stagnant water, covered in algae and leaves.

The key to moving downriver without hindrance is to stay in the flow of the current. I've rafted on some big rivers and I've tubed small ones. Either way, staying in the current makes the experience much more exhilarating. Have you ever sailed a toy boat down a river or paddled a canoe or kayak down a river? If you have, you know that staying in the current is what propels objects forward. The closer the object gets to the edge of the current, the more the likelihood of the object drifting, losing momentum, and even becoming stuck in the stagnant water on the sidelines of the current.

What is the life lesson here? We need to stay in the current because that is where the power of momentum is. We don't want to live our lives in the stagnant water where algae grow. Not that we can't work to get out of the stagnant area and back into the flow. We can, but it is much harder than just staying in the current, to begin with.

The powerful current I am referring to, spiritually speaking, is the power of the Living God. If we believe in Him, we have access to the full power of the Holy Spirit that operates in and through us. The more we read the Bible and learn the Scriptures, the more we will understand the power of God learn to flow with him. It is the powerful current of God and the flow of the Holy Spirit that will propel us forward.

Matthew 22:20 (NLT)*"Jesus replied, "Your mistake is that you don't know the Scriptures, and you don't know the power of God."*

Prayer: Lord, I pray that you reveal your power to me as I read the Bible and I pray that the power of the Holy Spirit is evident in me and around me and Protect me becoming stagnant in life.

Day Twenty-Five
Activity Levels

The level of activity you participate in on the river is your choice. Some people arrive on the river for a weekend and rush from one activity to another from the moment they arrive until the moment they leave. Fishing first thing in the morning, tubing and swimming before lunch, hikes along the bank searching for frogs and crayfish, followed by more fishing in the afternoon. As the day fades and darkness envelopes, the bonfire provides the perfect spot for storytelling until the wee hours.

Sleep is momentary before the first light of dawn appears and it is time to grab the pole and head back to the water in an effort to catch the elusive trophy fish.

Another may arrive at the river and determine to spend the weekend unwinding and enjoying the sights and sounds of the river from the Adirondack that sits perched atop the riverbank near a deep hole. The slight of a finger and the shutter snaps a picture of the heron gliding through the morning stillness in search of breakfast. The coffee mug sits on the arm of the chair, steam rising into the cool air as the shutter clicks in hopes of capturing the fish beginning to breach the surface. Silence is broken as fishermen arrive on the scene to begin their morning quest, and the onlooker retreats to the campsite to make breakfast.

On the surface, it may appear the first scenario is that of an active person and the second is one of inactivity. Yet, the second is also active, just differently.

Psalm 46:10 (NIV) says *"Be still and know I am God."* It was most likely David who asked God to lead him in Psalm 23:2-3 (NIV). *"...lead me beside the quiet waters and refresh my soul."*

Being still is contrary to the rat race of society that we have learned to function in. Sometimes, stepping away from the busyness of life and taking time to recharge your batteries at a slower pace is just what is needed. It has been said that we cannot love what we do not learn to linger over. Lingering at the river over a cup of coffee, watching the wildlife is a means of rejuvenating at a deeper level. May you linger today.

Prayer: Lord, teach me to linger here at the river and indeed as I live my day-to-day life. Teach me to slow down and allow you to refresh my soul.

Day Twenty-Six
Surviving or Thriving

What makes the difference between surviving and thriving? I submit it is several factors that play a contributing part in the ability to thrive. Have you ever looked the river banks during spring run-off? The plant life is lush and green, thriving in the warm air and water. Mighty oaks are beginning to leave out.

If you've taken a look at the same river banks during mid-summer when there is a drought going on you see a different situation. Once thriving shorter greenery is turning brown and struggling to survive, as the water table has made it difficult for roots to reach the necessary water source. Grasses have withered and died. Yet, there is the mighty oak, strong and green, continuing to thrive. How is this possible?

The mighty oak has an incredible root system which, while only eighteen inches below the surface, covers an area four to seven times the size of the tree canopy. The roots have smaller tentacles that intertwine, forming a dense net and strength. Larger trees can absorb up to 50 gallons of water a day, providing a reserve for days of drought.

If we are to thrive, Psalm 1:2 (NIV) tells us to be those *"Whose delight is in the law of the Lord, and who meditates on his law (Bible) day and night."*

The promise is found in Psalm 1:3 (NIV), which likens us to the mighty oak and instructs us on how we can thrive in life. *"That person is like a tree planted by streams of water, which yields its fruit in season and whose leaf does not wither--whatever they do prospers."*

If you want to be strong and able to handle any of the storms (circumstances) of life, and be able to thrive in the midst of the challenges, you've got to let your roots grow deep. I speak experientially when I say you can thrive in the midst of a health crisis, financial challenges, or broken relationships.

Prayer: Lord, I pray you teach me your ways and give me the desire to implement your ways in my daily life that I may be like the mighty oak and thrive, despite the storms of life that come my way. I know I was not created to merely survive, barely hanging on each time a drought or storm comes. Your way is better and I commit to finding my delight in you.

Day Twenty-Seven
Sit in Awe

Have you ever taken the time to just sit and watch the river and be in awe of it? If not, perhaps today is the day to do it! Whether it happens to be a high water day or a low water day, the river is a wondrous body of water teeming with life. It is an awesome thing to ponder how the water moves swiftly across the rocks in the middle while lying stagnant in the coves of the river bank.

The powerful current can carry two people in a raft across the rapids, but fish can maintain their position without being carried downstream. For hour after endless hours, water swirls around vegetation in the crevice of rock yet does not uproot it. When one takes the time to sit and closely observe the ways of the river, awe is a certain response.

The same holds when we take the time to slow down and observe details of the Creator of the river and life therein. Exodus 15:11 (Amp) says *"Who is like You among the gods, O Lord? Who is like You, majestic in holiness, awesome in splendor, working wonders?"*

Psalm 33:8 (NASB) says *"Let all the earth fear the Lord and all the inhabitants of the world stand in awe of Him."*

Consider the ways of God. Not just in His creation, but in how He works in our lives. Have you ever said a quick prayer and gotten an answer almost immediately? We should not be quick to overlook the awe of the moment, that the Creator of the universe cares enough about us (of the billions on the planet) to hear and answer our prayers. If you are like me, life gets busy and you just don't always slow down enough to ponder the wonder of it all. Determine to change that and to slow down and soak in the awesomeness of the river of God.

Prayer: God, I ask that you would teach me to slow down and to truly ponder your majesty and awesomeness. Not just in the world, you've created but your displays of wonderworking splendor. May I never cease to sit in awe of you.

Day Twenty-Eight
Community in the River

We all yearn for community. We were created for community. No living being is created to live in isolation. If you consider all of the creatures living in the river, you will find community within the diversity. Different types of fish are sharing the same waters. Not only is there a variety of fish but there are also turtles, frogs, crayfish, birds, various insects, and other life living in the river community.

Not all creatures dwell well together. While diversity has its place, some river dwellers are predators who need to be avoided. You've heard the saying "Birds of a feather flock together". The same holds true for certain species of fish.

Smaller fish are the prey of the larger fish. To stay safe, the smaller fish live in community with one another and keep a respectable distance from the larger fish. Just as fish school and birds flock, people gravitate toward one another. All living things need a community in which to thrive. Not all people think and believe the same and while diversity is important, there is a need for also developing a community of like-minded believers.

Finding a community that believes in Jesus can mean finding just one other person, or can mean finding dozens at a worship service. We need one another for encouragement and companionship. We don't always need to have large numbers of people to form a valuable community. In Matthew 18:20 (NASB)Jesus said *"Where two or three are gathered in my name, there I am in the midst of them."*

Many times, it is a small group gathering that forms a sense of community. Sometimes we gather for a church service, such as was done in Acts 13:44 (NASB) "The next Sabbath, nearly the whole city gathered to hear the Word of the Lord." We are instructed not to forsake assembling together as a community of believers. Hebrews 10:25 (NASB) *"Let us not abandoning our own meeting together, as is the habit of some people, but encouraging one another; and all the more as you see the day drawing near."*

Prayer: Lord, I know there is community in the family of Believers (in Christ) that is different than the community I find at my workplace or even in my own family. I acknowledge my need for being in community with those who know you. Help me to develop relationships in a community of like-minded people.

Day Twenty-Nine
Be Prepared

As surely as day turns to night and back to day again, rains will come and the waters will rise again and then fall again. Such is the way of the river. Fishermen know when the fish will be biting and plan their weekend accordingly. When an inch or two of rain is forecast, avid river rafters start preparing and clear their calendar for the following day, knowing the waters will be swift and they'll have a good run.

Wisdom says that we need to be prepared for the storms that living life brings. While we cannot know for certain when and which personal storms will come, the reality is that most of us will face undesirable situations periodically throughout our time on this earth. For some, it is the unwelcome diagnosis of a disease. For others, it is the news of a financial disaster.

How do we prepare? There are the practical aspects of preparation, such as creating an emergency savings account or doing all we know to do to live a healthy lifestyle. It is wise to consider how we can be prepared for circumstances we may find ourselves in. Proverbs 22:3 (ESV) says "*A prudent man sees danger and hides himself, but the simple go on and suffer for it.*"

The most important preparation, however, is to be prepared to face our own death. While we may escape a financial disaster or disease that others face, the truth is none of us will escape death. Are you prepared? Regardless of your current age, are you ready? I don't mean to suggest you have to live on guard, always wondering "Is today the day?" As my wise aunt used to tell me "Live every day as if it is your last, because one day you will be right." Knowing Jesus Christ and living as He expects us to will keep us in a state of continual readiness.

Ecclesiastes 9:12 (CEB)"*People most definitely don't know when their time will come. Like fish tragically caught in a net or birds trapped in a snare, so are human beings tragically caught in a time that suddenly falls to them.*"

Prayer: Lord God, help me to be better prepared for the natural circumstances that arise in life, help me to live each day in a way of preparation to end my time on this earth and enter eternity, knowing my salvation is secure and I will abide with you in heaven forever.

Day Thirty

Experience the River

There are those who jump into the river and enjoy all there is to offer: tubing, swimming, fishing, soaking in the natural jets (rapids), searching for lost treasures, and living creatures. Others sit on the riverbank wistful, watching, and having the desire to join in the fun, yet never taking the steps necessary to do so. While some will rest at the river, others will not find rest.

Reasons vary as to why bystanders sit on the riverbanks watching and never experience the joy of the river or find rest there. Some are skeptical and wonder if it's worth the effort, some fearful of the unknowns about the river. They spend their entire time at the river without ever actually experiencing it for themselves. To me, this is a tragedy of life. To have such a treasure right there all of the time, a gift with no limits for whosoever will, and yet never partake of all to be found there.

Think of the river as a banquet table. There are many options at one table. It is a feast, for whosoever is willing to partake. There are those who will come as soon as the invitation is extended and will freely partake of all that is offered.

There are those who accept the invitation more of curiosity than anything else and will decline to partake of little if any of what is laid before them, and there are those who decline the invitation, much like those invited to the banquet spoken of in Luke 14. The river is filled with abundant life and is meant to be partaken of, not to be enjoyed from afar.

Revelation 22:17b (ESV) *"And let the one who is thirsty come; let the one who desires take the water of life without price."*

Prayer: Lord, I am thirsty and in need of a drink from you, the Living Water. I do not want to live life watching others partake of all you have to offer, always wondering what it would be like if I would only have the courage to enjoy all you offer. May Rivers of Living Water flow in and through me.

Life in Jesus, Plain and Simple

Does all of this talk about Jesus leave you confused? Maybe you've never been to church or the church you go to doesn't teach you that of the need to have a personal relationship with Jesus Christ. Let me explain it, plain and simple.

God loves you. He created you for a purpose to fulfill here on earth before going to be in heaven with Him. (Read Genesis 1 & 2) There can be no sin (wrongs) allowed in heaven because God is pure and holy. Unfortunately for all of us, Adam and Eve sinned by disobeying God in the Garden of Eden (You probably know the story-Genesis 3).

Once perfect mankind became sinful and to this day we all sin (do wrong), sometimes intentionally and sometimes without thinking. Maybe you said an unkind thing to someone. Maybe a little white lie was told. Maybe you stole an extra 15 minutes from your boss by taking a long coffee break. Those things are all wrong, which God calls sin.

Remember, God created you to live in heaven but sin cannot be in heaven. The penalty of sin is death unless an acceptable payment is made. In the Old Testament, people offered sacrifices to God to ask for forgiveness and make payment for the sins committed.

Obviously, that gets tedious! The great news is that Jesus came from heaven to earth in the form of a baby and lived a sinless, perfect life here on earth for 33 years. When He was crucified as the Ultimate Sacrifice, He willingly paid for our sins for the remainder of eternity. God the Father accepted the sacrifice His son Jesus made.

What is your part now, if Jesus already paid the sacrifice for you? You must believe He is the Christ, the son of the Living God, who was born here on earth in the form of a baby and lived here fully God, yet fully man. You must believe that He was crucified, then buried, and then miraculously and supernaturally rose from the dead on the third day. (Mark 16:6) This is the Resurrection/Easter Story. The Book of Acts gives at least 12 accounts of Jesus appearing after the Resurrection, to more than 500 people. When He ascended back to Heaven, He said He was going to prepare a place for us, that we might have eternal life.

The amazing thing about eternal life is that it is a free gift given to us by God through faith alone and not by any of our good deeds (Ephesians 2:8-9). Jesus paid the price for our sins when He died on the cross and all we must do is receive the gift of forgiveness through faith. When we believe that Jesus died for our sins and trust in Him alone we receive eternal life, are passed out of death into life, and are guaranteed a home in heaven (John 5:24).

Most of us have heard John 3:16-which speaks plain and simple. *"For God so loved the world that he gave his one and only Son, that whoever believes in him shall not perish but have eternal life."* It's literally that simplistic. You just need to believe.

Still skeptical? Maybe you aren't really believing there is just one True God who is alive and powerful? Maybe you don't believe Jesus is real and living in heaven, seated at the right hand of God, the Father. Perhaps you need more evidence?

To me, the best evidence of there being a Creator is nature. Stop for a few moments and look at nature. Many would tell you what you see is the result of a 'Big Bang' or evolution? Do you really believe that? Ponder the different species of plants and animals that are visible just within your sight. Do you honestly think everything just evolved? Or there was some cosmic 'bang' and then everything just somehow magically came together and boom-a fish appeared? Boom-there's a bird? Boom, a turtle. BAM-a person? Not likely.

If not evolution or a bang, then there must be someone who created all of this, wouldn't you agree? The question then remains of who the Creator is. According to the Bible, the Creator is God. (Reread Genesis) If you are going to believe God created this amazing universe filled with so much variety of living things, you are acknowledging truths only known to us because it is written in the Bible.

There is lots of information on how you can research the authenticity of the Bible, of Jesus' life and miracles on earth, and of the assurance that He indeed is the Messiah, the one many are still waiting for to come to rescue them.

No one is born knowing about Jesus. We only know what we've been taught in some type of church or what is generally believed and discussed in society. Sadly, the majority will not research and read the Bible for themselves. They often accept and read variations filled with additions and omissions that have been given to them.

I'm not saying you need to get your Doctorate as I did, but I am saying that you owe it to yourself to find out the truth. Read the Bible with your own eyes. Ask questions. Find the answers.

Believe in your heart that Jesus is who He says He is (The Son of God the Father) and that He came to earth born as a baby, lived, was crucified, rose again on the third day, and thereby paid the penalty of your sins and allowing you to escape eternal death you deserve for all of the wrongs you've done and will do in life. Once you believe these truths, you need to ask Him to forgive you of your sins, thank Him for paying the price for you, that you may have eternal life in heaven with Him.

After asking Him to forgive you and to become the Savior you need, you need to begin to allow Him to be the Captain of your ship, the Director of your decisions and life, the Person who decides what you should and should not be doing. With the help of the Holy Spirit, you will discover these things as you read the Bible, pray, and learn.

The lessons spoken of in this little book, learned by observing the river, will make more sense to you as time goes on and you get better acquainted with Jesus, who provides the Living Water. It is my prayer that you find the exceedingly abundant life that God created you to have and that you overflow with purpose and joy and all good things found when living a life in Jesus.

Blessings to you!

Mel

About Mel

Born and raised in Maine, Mel later moved to Connecticut. She is married, mother to seven adult children and ten grands. Her desire is that you be equipped to live an abundant purpose-filled life.

Dr. Tavares serves on staff in the Pastoral Care and Counseling Ministry in her church. She is the author of several books, including *Equipping Families to Thrive in Today's Youth Culture* and *Return to Eden: Exposing the Lies that are Destroying the Family*. She is a contributing writer for Inspiration Ministries and for DaySpring's "*Sweet Tea for the Grieving Soul*". Mel writes a weekly blog on her website, focused on equipping Christians to thrive in life.

Contact Info
Email: drmeltavares@gmail.com
Website: drmeltavares.com

Made in the USA
Monee, IL
06 April 2021